A Note to Parents

DK READ... ...ing
readers, de... ...ng literacy

experts, including Dr. Linda Gambrell, Professor of Education
at Clemson University. Dr. Gambrell has served as President
of the National Reading Conference and the College
Reading Association, and has recently been elected to serve
as President of the International Reading Association.

Beautiful illustrations and superb full-color photographs
combine with engaging, easy-to-read stories to offer a fresh
approach to each subject in the series. Each DK READER is
guaranteed to capture a child's interest while developing his
or her reading skills, general knowledge, and love of reading.

The five levels of DK READERS are aimed at different
reading abilities, enabling you to choose the books that are
exactly right for your child:

Pre-level 1: Learning to read
Level 1: Beginning to read
Level 2: Beginning to read alone
Level 3: Reading alone
Level 4: Proficient readers

The "normal" age at which a child begins to read can be
anywhere from three to eight years old. Adult participation
through the lower levels is very helpful for providing
encouragement, discussing storylines, and sounding out
unfamiliar words.

No matter which level you select, you
can be sure that you are helping your
child learn to read, then read to learn!

LONDON, NEW YORK, MUNICH,
MELBOURNE, AND DELHI

Editor Hannah Dolan
Designer Rhys Thomas
Senior Designer Rob Perry
Managing Art Editor Ron Stobbart
Art Director Lisa Lanzarini
Publishing Manager Catherine Saunders
Associate Publisher Simon Beecroft
Category Publisher Alex Allan
Production Editor Clare McLean
Production Controller Nick Seston

Reading Consultant
Linda B. Gambrell, Ph.D.

First published in the United States in 2011
by DK Publishing
375 Hudson Street, New York, New York 10014

12 13 14 15 10 9 8 7 6 5

006-176218-Feb/2011

DK books are available at special discounts when purchased in bulk
for sales promotions, premiums, fund-raising, or educational use.
For details, contact:
DK Publishing Special Markets
375 Hudson Street
New York, New York 10014
SpecialSales@dk.com

A catalog record for this book is available
from the Library of Congress.

ISBN: 978-0-7566-7706-0 (Paperback)
ISBN: 978-0-7566-7707-7 (Hardcover)

Color reproduction by MDP
Printed and bound in China by L-Rex

Discover more at
www.dk.com

www.LEGO.com

DK READERS

BEGINNING
1
TO READ

Brickbeard's Treasure

Written by Hannah Dolan

Ahoy, me hearty!
That means "Hello, my friend!"
to a pirate.
This fierce pirate is called
Captain Brickbeard.

He is the captain of this ship.
It is called *Brickbeard's Bounty*.

Captain Brickbeard
and his crew sail
the high seas in
Brickbeard's Bounty.

treasure

They are always looking for treasure and adventure. Let's go aboard the ship and have a look around!

Look at the top of the ship and you will see a black flag.

flag

The flag has a skull
and some bones on it.
It is called the Jolly Roger.
It will scare the pirates'
enemies away!

Can you see the pretty
mermaid on the ship?
She is called a figurehead.
The pirates hope that she
will bring the ship good
luck in stormy seas and
shark-filled waters!

figurehead

The ship has powerful cannons. The pirates use them when they do battle with their enemies. The pirates' enemies are other treasure-seekers on the high seas!

The soldiers of the King's Navy protect the high seas from pirates. They are always looking for pirates who are up to no good!

The King's soldiers are the pirates' biggest enemies.

Sometimes the King's soldiers take the pirates' treasure.

Sometimes the pirates steal theirs!

What's this? One of the pirates has found an old treasure map! The cross on it tells him where treasure is buried.

This soldier wants the map, too.

Look out!

He is firing cannon balls
with his big cannon!

An old pirate is guarding
treasure on this island.
His pirate ship left
him behind!

The pirates and the King's
soldiers have found the
treasure!
Who will
reach it first?

These pirates have some treasure!
They are on a wooden raft.
The raft floats along very slowly.
The pirates are taking their
treasure to *Brickbeard's Bounty*.

raft

This sea monster is another
enemy of the pirates!
It loves shiny treasure, too.
It has eight arms to help it steal
the pirates' treasure!

The pirates must keep their treasure safe. They hide it in their secret hideout. It has hidden traps to scare away enemies!

Look out, pirates!
These soldiers
have found your hideout!

This is the King's Navy's fortress.
It is where the King's soldiers
keep their treasure safe.

fortress

Look! Captain Brickbeard wants
to steal the soldiers' treasure!

The fortress has a prison cell.
The soldiers have locked up a
pirate in the prison cell.
Look who is here to rescue him!

prison cell

Captain Brickbeard's clever pet monkey is trained to steal things. He steals the key to the prison cell and sets the pirate free!

Now you know all about
pirates, you could be one too.
You can enjoy your own
pirate adventures!

"Goodbye, me hearty," says Captain Brickbeard.

Glossary

page 6

treasure

page 8

flag

page 10

figurehead

page 20

raft

page 26

fortress

page 28

prison cell

Beyond the Sky

by **ANNA PROKOS**
With the Editors of TIME For Kids

Table of Contents

Chapter 1
Eye on the Sky 2

Chapter 2
Dizzy Planet 4

Chapter 3
Follow the Sun 6

Chapter 4
Star Watch 8

Chapter 5
To the Moon! 12

Glossary .15

Index 16

Eye on the Sky

What do you see when you look up at the sky? In the day, you may see the Sun. At night, you may see the Moon and the **stars**.

Sun | Venus | Earth | Mars | Jupiter | Saturn | Uranus | Neptune

The Sun, the Moon, and the stars are part of the **solar system**. Eight planets are in the solar system, too. Earth is the only planet with plants and animals. It has the right mix of **gases** and water for living things.

The Sun is at the center of the solar system. Earth travels around the Sun. This path is called an **orbit**. As Earth moves around the Sun, it also spins.

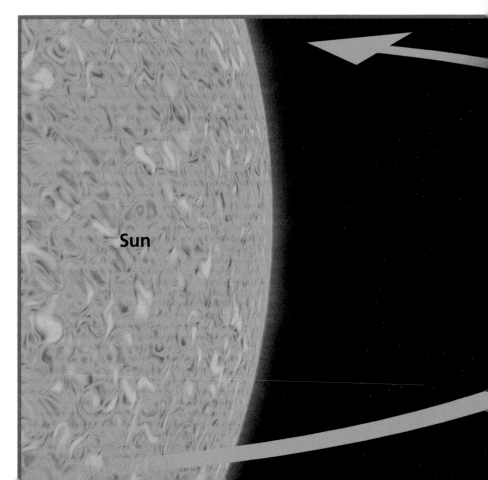

Sun

4

How can you tell Earth is spinning? Look at things you can see beyond our sky. They are the Sun, the Moon, and the stars. They seem to move across the sky. But what really is moving is Earth!

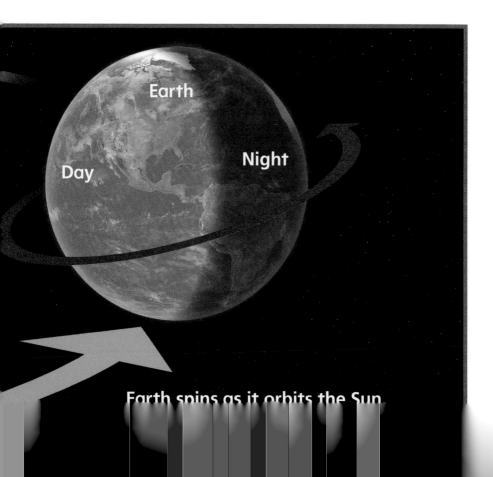

Earth

Day

Night

Earth spins as it orbits the Sun.

Chapter 3

Follow the Sun

Watch the Sun. In the early morning, it is low in the sky. In the middle of the day, it is high in the sky. Later in the day, the Sun is lower on the other side of the sky. Finally, the Sun sets. It is night.

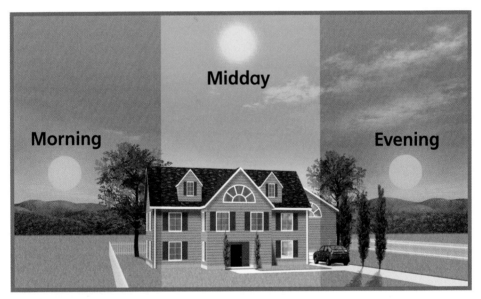

This shows the movement of the Sun from morning to evening.

When your place on Earth is turned to the Sun, you have day. As Earth spins, your place moves to the Sun's light. You go through morning and afternoon. Then your place turns away from the Sun. It is night. But Earth keeps turning until your place moves back into the Sun's light. It is morning again!

Chapter 4

Star Watch

There are millions of stars in space. Yet you can see only about a thousand stars at night. The rest are too far away. You need a **telescope** to see them.

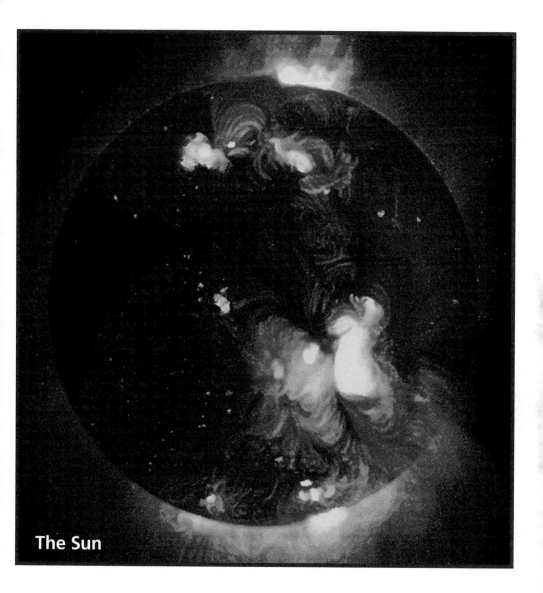

The Sun

A star is a giant ball of burning gas. As the gas burns, it sends light and heat into space. The Sun is a star. It is the star closest to Earth. Heat and light from the Sun make it possible for us to live on Earth.

Earth is just the right distance from the Sun. If it were closer, Earth would be too hot and burn. The oceans would boil.

If Earth were farther away from the Sun, plants, animals, and people would freeze.

Stars

Stars might look alike from Earth.
Yet they come in many sizes and colors.

Type of Star	Color	Size
White dwarf	White	Tiny for a star— about the size of Earth
Red dwarf	Red	Smaller than the Sun
Yellow dwarf	Yellow	Medium size— about the size of the Sun
Blue giant	Blue	Bigger than the Sun
Supergiant	Red or orange	200 times bigger than the Sun

Chapter 5

To the Moon!

The Moon is not a star. It doesn't make its own light. We see the Moon because the Sun's light is shining on it. It is like shining a flashlight on the side of a house in the dark. You see only the part that is lit up by the flashlight.

Sometimes, the Moon looks like a big round ball. On other nights, it has a different shape. Sometimes we cannot see the Moon at all. These changes are called the **phases** of the Moon.

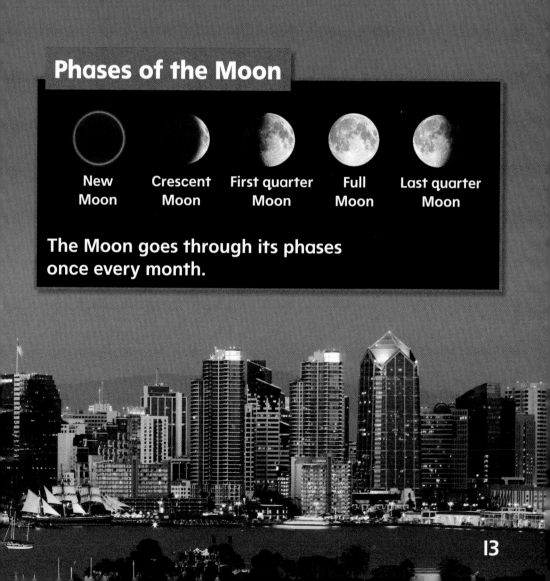

Phases of the Moon

| New Moon | Crescent Moon | First quarter Moon | Full Moon | Last quarter Moon |

The Moon goes through its phases once every month.

The Sun, the Moon, and the stars are in the space beyond our sky. What do you think is beyond the Sun, the Moon, and the stars?

Glossary

 gas (GAS) matter that spreads out to fill all the space it is in *(page 3)*

 orbit (OR-bit) the path of a planet traveling around a star *(page 4)*

 phase (FAYZ) the Moon's shape we can see from Earth *(page 13)*

 solar system (SOH-luhr SIS-tuhm) the planets and other objects that go around the Sun *(page 3)*

 star (STAR) a hot ball in the sky that makes its own light *(page 2)*

 telescope (TEL-uh-skohp) a tool used to see things far away *(page 8)*

Index

Earth, 3–5, 7, 9, 10–11

gas, 3, 9

Moon, 2–3, 5, 12–14

orbit, 3

phases of the Moon, 13

planet, 3

solar system, 3–4

star, 2–3, 5, 8–9, 11–12, 14

Sun, 2–7, 9–10, 12, 14

telescope, 8